Rocks
and
Fossils

Written and edited by Martyn Bramwell
Consultant Alan Woolley
Designed by Sylvia Tate

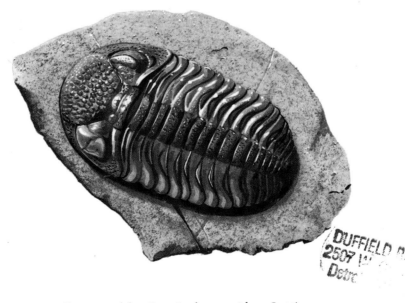

Illustrated by Ian Jackson, Alan Suttie,
Mike Saunders (Tudor Art), Elaine Keenan,
David McGrail, Ann Winterbotham, Aziz Khan, Rob McCaig,
David Wright (Jillian Burgess), Steve Lings (Linden Artists),
Chris Shields (Wilcock Riley), Nigel Frey

One of the greatest detective stories of all time is the story of how man has unravelled the history of our planet earth. Every time we step out of doors we are surrounded by clues. The shape of the countryside, the rocks, and the minerals and fossils they contain, the rivers, glaciers, winds and oceans, and even the plant and animal life around us – all have something to tell. This book explains what the earth is made of and describes the forces that are constantly changing it. It looks at many of the most common rocks, minerals and fossils, and explains how to find them, identify them, and understand them. Nearly two hundred years ago, the great geologist Sir Charles Lyell said, 'The present is the key to the past'. Ever since then, geologists have been piecing together the clues. We now understand a great deal about our planet's history. But many discoveries still await the next generation of young geologists.

The rock-hunter's code

- Stick to footpaths and the edges of fields when crossing farmland.

- Keep your dog under control. It may be tempted to chase animals.

- Use gates and stiles instead of scrambling over walls. Always close gates to protect farm animals.

- Take your litter home. It looks awful and is a danger to animals.

- Always tell somebody where you are going, and when you will be back.

- Take special care near cliffs and loose rocks, and at the seashore.

- Wear goggles to protect your eyes when hammering. And never break off more rock than really necessary.

- Don't be tempted to explore caves and potholes. They are dangerous.

Things to do

Look for the hand-lens symbol. It spotlights practical experiments and other projects that you can do at home and in the country. The experiments can all be done without special equipment and will help you understand how geology shapes our world. You can identify minerals and fossils, make time charts, show how geological processes work, and build up collections.

Contents

Scenery

Discover the art of 'reading' the landscape around you. It is full of clues that tell you what rocks it is made of and what geological processes have carved it into the hills and valleys, mountains and deserts you see today.

Minerals

Take a close look at minerals and crystals – the amazing variety of colours and shapes that make up nature's building blocks. Grow your own crystals, and find out how to identify the most common minerals and build up a collection.

Rocks

Learn about the great 'families' of rocks – how they are made, where they come from, where to find them and how to recognize them. Discover the geology of your town or city by looking at the buildings and statues and find out how to explore the countryside around you.

Fossils

Explore the animal and plant life of the earth's distant past by using the clues left behind in the rocks. See how fossils were formed and how they have recorded the evolution of life on earth. Learn how to collect, identify and preserve your finds.

Geologists at work

Look into the world of the professional geologists – the sort of work they do, and why their work affects our everyday life. Find out about drilling for oil, prospecting for minerals, and predicting earthquakes. See how transparent slices of rock are examined under the microscope and discover why some of the smallest (and most beautiful) fossils are so important.

Discovering the past

The oldest written history books go back only a few thousand years – not much more than a blink of an eye on the geological time-scale. But we can still discover what the earth was like before man arrived. For nearly 4,600 million years our planet has been keeping its own records, and the whole story is 'written' in the rocks of the earth's crust.

From rocks and fossils we know that dinosaurs once ruled the earth, that insects flew on wings spanning 30cm, that Europe was once on the equator and that swamp forests grew in Antarctica. Unravelling the clues is not always easy – but every rock has something to tell us.

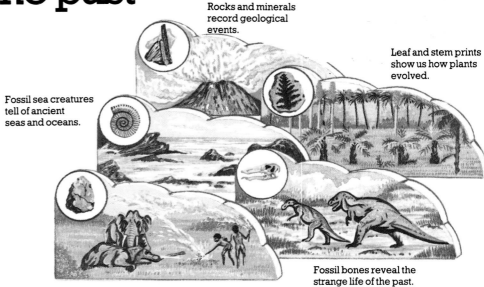

Rocks and minerals record geological events.

Leaf and stem prints show us how plants evolved.

Fossil sea creatures tell of ancient seas and oceans.

There are even clues to how ancient man hunted.

Fossil bones reveal the strange life of the past.

Looking for rocks and fossils

Mountain country usually has plenty of bare rock and loose stones, and you may even be able to see places where rocks have been broken or bent into folds. **Cliffs** too are ideal places to collect rocks and fossils. Piles of **fallen rock** at the base of a cliff are good places to search, but don't forget to look carefully at the **beach** **pebbles** as well; some may have come long distances. **River banks** and **road cuttings** are always good hunting grounds. So too are **quarries,** but you must ask permission before you enter in case blasting is in progress. Stay well away from machinery. Never be tempted to explore abandoned mines.

Geology on your doorstep

Look at the buildings in your town. Many will be made of local stone but banks, town halls, libraries and public monuments are often made of beautiful imported stones. Look out for different types of marble, granite, limestone and other decorative stones.

Look at the walls, altar, font and gravestones in your local churches. You may find quite a variety of local and imported stones.

Statues and memorials are ofte carved from fine white marble

Polished granite is often used in banks and office buildings.

Use this book to help you identify the stones you find. See if you can find out where they came from, then plot your finds on a map of the town, with sketches and notes. (What effect has city air had on the different types of stone?)

Collecting your specimens

Hunting for rocks and fossils is great fun, but be careful not to take risks. Hammering at the base of a cliff may bring down loose rock – so stay back. There is always plenty of fallen rock to work on. Use your hammer to break off a fresh specimen. Then number it with a felt pen and describe it in your note-book, with a note of just where you found it. Wrap it in newspaper to avoid scratching it on the way home.

Goggles will protect your eyes from dust and rock fragments.

Buy a proper geologist's hammer. (An ordinary hammer is no good.)

Wear boots and strong, old, outdoor clothes as you will probably end up quite dirty. If you are going out for the day, especially in the hills, take food and a hot drink, and always tell someone exactly where you are going.

Use a folding lens with a magnification of ×8 or ×10. Hold it close to your eye, then bring the specimen into focus with the other hand.

Strong back-pack

Food and drink

Local map

Field-guides

Newspapers for wrapping specimens

Notebook and felt pens

Don't be shy. Get in close and use your lens. Try to identify any minerals or fossils that are visible.

History repeats itself

In May 1980 a huge volcanic eruption blew the top 400 metres off Mount St Helens in North America. Five hundred square kilometres of forest were flattened by the blast, and the area was blanketed with fine volcanic ash.

Ten million years ago a similar blast shook the western United States. But it was perhaps a hundred times bigger. In what is now Nebraska, three-toed horses, rhinos, camels and deer were caught unawares at a waterhole. Choked by the gritty dust they died in their hundreds. First ash, then river sands, covered them over – hiding the disaster until fossil hunters made their exciting discovery in 1978.

You may not make discoveries as exciting as this one – but there are plenty of fossils to find, and each one tells its own story.

Mountains on the move

The earth, the moon and the planets are made up mainly of materials we call rocks. And these in turn are made up of collections of natural substances called minerals. There are dozens of different rock types but each can be placed in one of the three main rock 'families'. Igneous rocks develop from molten material deep inside the earth. Sedimentary rocks consist of the worn-down fragments of other rocks. And metamorphic rocks (the name means 'change') are formed when older rocks are altered by heat and pressure into new rocks. The diagram opposite shows how all these rocks are part of a never-ending cycle of change. The processes are very slow. They may take hundreds of millions of years. But nothing in nature remains unchanged for long.

Frost and ice, wind and rain, and chemicals dissolved in rainwater, break down the rocks into small fragments.

There are marine fossils at 6,700 metres on Mt Everest.

Inside the earth

The 'solid' earth beneath our feet is really just a thin cool crust: 50km down the temperature is about 800°C and deeper still, at about 2,000km, the temperature is probably well over 2,200°C. At this depth the rocks behave more like liquids.

Light continental rocks float on top of denser layers, and mountain ranges are buoyed up by deep roots – rather like wooden blocks floating in water.

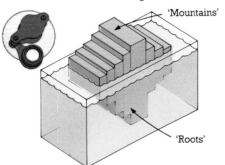

'Mountains'

'Roots'

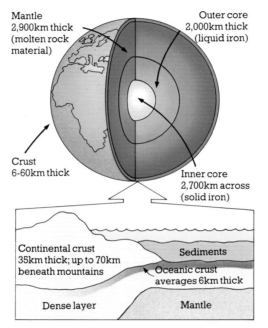

Mantle 2,900km thick (molten rock material)

Outer core 2,000km thick (liquid iron)

Crust 6-60km thick

Inner core 2,700km across (solid iron)

Continental crust 35km thick; up to 70km beneath mountains

Sediments

Oceanic crust averages 6km thick

Dense layer

Mantle

Complex geological processes cause the land to rise farther above sea level. And so the cycle starts all over again with the frost, wind and rain.

The wandering continents

We now know that as well as 'floating' on the deeper mantle rocks, continents can move about the earth's surface like huge rafts. The 'jigsaw' fit of the continents puzzled scientists for many years, and the idea of continental drift has only been proved correct during the past 20 years.

Computers have been used to help plot maps of the continents as they would have appeared millions of years ago. The land masses have drifted, collided, joined together and then broken apart again. We can even plot where they are likely to be millions of years in the future.

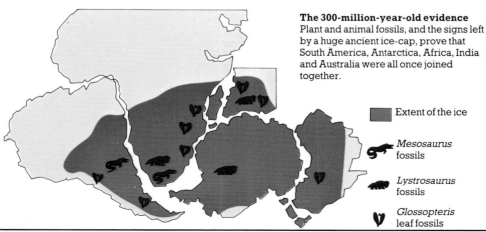

The 300-million-year-old evidence
Plant and animal fossils, and the signs left by a huge ancient ice-cap, prove that South America, Antarctica, Africa, India and Australia were all once joined together.

Extent of the ice

Mesosaurus fossils

Lystrosaurus fossils

Glossopteris leaf fossils

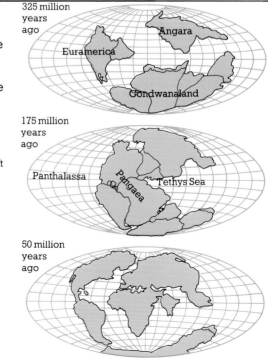

325 million years ago

Angara

Euramerica

Gondwanaland

175 million years ago

Panthalassa

Pangaea

Tethys Sea

50 million years ago

Streams, rivers, glaciers and sudden flash floods in the desert carry the worn-down fragments towards the sea.

Glaciers dump piles of boulder clay and rivers build up sand and pebble banks, but most of the material ends up in the sea.

Rainfall feeds the rivers.

Wind-blown sand carves strange desert landscapes.

Winds carry fine dust far out to sea.

Coarse sand sinks first, near the land, while finer mud and silt is carried farther out to sea. After millions of years, the weight of hundreds of metres of sediment squeezes out most of the water. Chemical changes take place and the sediment becomes rock.

Pressure and intense heat change some sediments into new kinds of rock. Rising magma adds new rock to the cycle.

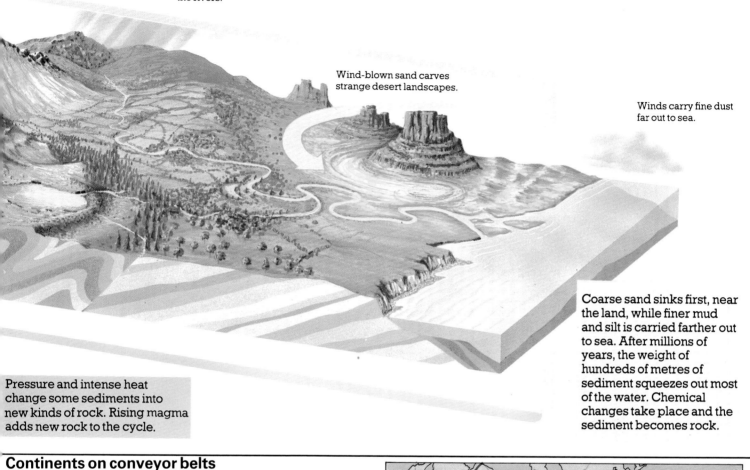

Continents on conveyor belts

What forces could possibly move whole continents? The answers came from studies of seabed geology. Long mountain ridges were found in the middle of the Atlantic and other oceans, and it was discovered that new ocean crust is being formed at the ridges all the time. The sea bed spreads away from the ridge like a conveyor belt, carrying huge 'rafts' of continental crust. The earth is not getting bigger so to compensate for the new crust, old crust is being dragged down into the mantle at other plate edges. These areas are marked by island arcs and mountain ranges and by volcanoes, earthquakes and deep ocean trenches.

—— Crust forming
—— Crust disappearing

① Volcanic island arc (Japan, Philippines)

Active volcanoes

② Mid-ocean ridge (East Pacific Rise)

③ Offshore trench and coastal mountain chain (Andes)

④ Remains of an ancient continental collision (Himalayas)

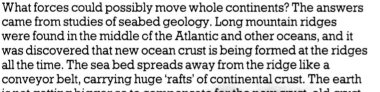

Crust melts at great depth

Magma wells up gently

Earthquakes form in this region

Ancient mountain roots

Rocks from inside the earth

Intrusive rocks

Instead of reaching the surface, rising magma may force its way in between other rocks and harden there as 'igneous intrusions'. Magma that hardened in the pipe of a volcano may remain long after surrounding rocks have worn away.

Le Puys, France. The pipe of an old volcano.

Igneous rocks are formed by the cooling of molten rock. They come from deep inside the earth's mantle, between 100 and 200 kilometres down, at a temperature of more than 1,500°C. This molten material is called magma. When it comes to the surface through a volcanic opening (a vent) it is called lava. Very fluid (runny) lava may spread over hundreds of square kilometres. Layers of stiffer lava, alternating with layers of volcanic ash, form steep-sided volcanoes like Kilimanjaro in Africa and Fujiyama in Japan. Some eruptions are explosive and cause great damage; others are quite gentle.

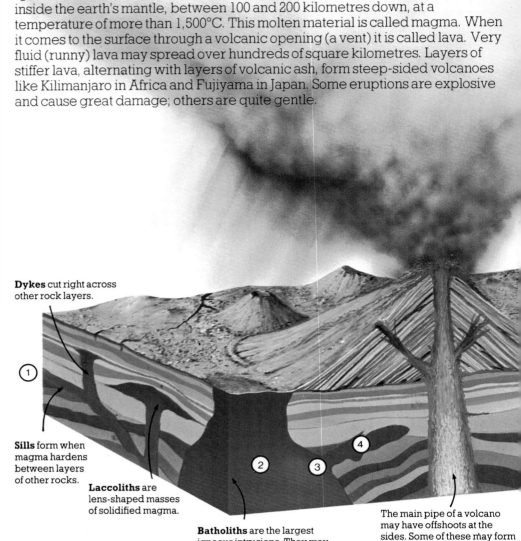

Dykes cut right across other rock layers.

Sills form when magma hardens between layers of other rocks.

Laccoliths are lens-shaped masses of solidified magma.

Batholiths are the largest igneous intrusions. They may extend over hundreds of square kilometres.

The main pipe of a volcano may have offshoots at the sides. Some of these may form small secondary volcanoes.

① Dolerite (Diabase)
Dark, medium-grained rock, usually found in sills and dykes. With a lens you will see light feldspar crystals and dark pyroxene crystals.

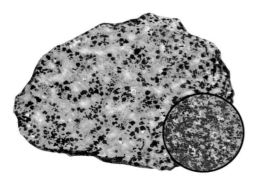

② Granite
Coarse-grained rock with good-sized crystals of glassy quartz, white or pink feldspar, dark mica and sometimes a black mineral, called hornblende.

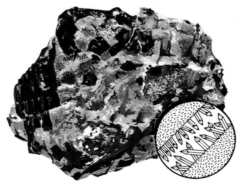

③ Pegmatite
Found in dykes and veins, usually in or near granite. Best source of large crystals; quartz, feldspar, mica and many other minerals form in cavities.

④ Quartz porphyry
Fine-grained lava or dyke rock with scattered large crystals of quartz and feldspar. Found in sills, dykes and old volcanic pipes.

When volcanic ash hardens, it forms a rock called 'tuff'. This may contain larger fragments called 'bombs'.

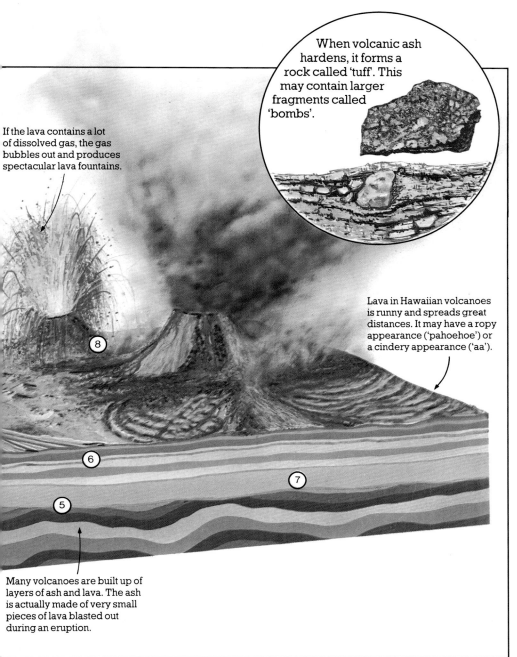

If the lava contains a lot of dissolved gas, the gas bubbles out and produces spectacular lava fountains.

⑧

⑥

⑤

⑦

Lava in Hawaiian volcanoes is runny and spreads great distances. It may have a ropy appearance ('pahoehoe') or a cindery appearance ('aa').

Many volcanoes are built up of layers of ash and lava. The ash is actually made of very small pieces of lava blasted out during an eruption.

Extrusive rocks

'Extrusive' means 'forced out' so this group contains all the lavas. Lava flows may cover huge areas and be hundreds of metres thick. Basalt lava may cool very slowly and form six-sided columns like those of the Giant's Causeway, Northern Ireland.

Geode with amethyst crystals

⑧ **Basalt**
Very dark. Too fine-grained to see crystals (except occasional dark green olivine). Cavities (geodes) sometimes contain superb crystals.

Banded agate

⑤ **Andesite**
Fine-grained grey, brown, purplish or black rock. Main minerals are feldspar, pyroxene and hornblende. May have cavities filled with banded agate.

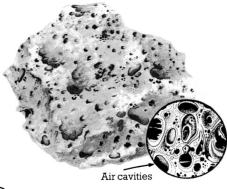

Air cavities

⑥ **Pumice**
Formed when lots of dissolved gas suddenly bubbles out of a lava. A solidified 'rock froth'. Unmistakable. The only rock that floats in water!

Obsidian arrow-head

⑦ **Obsidian**
Lava that cooled so quickly that crystals had no time to form. Black or greenish volcanic glass. The shell-like fracture produces sharp edges.

From sediment to stone

Most of the earth's surface is covered with loose material called sediment. It may be soil in a garden, mud in a river, or the sand and pebbles on a beach. Geological processes turn these loose sediments into sedimentary rocks. But sedimentary rocks can also be formed in other ways. Some, like rock salt and some limestones, are formed from minerals dissolved in water. Others, like coal, chalk and shelly limestones, are made from the remains of plants and animals that lived millions of years ago. The layers, or beds, are an important feature of sedimentary rocks.

Limestones

Limestones may form from calcium carbonate dissolved in the waters of warm, shallow seas. Sometimes the mineral accumulates in tiny balls called ooliths, which are later cemented together to make oolitic limestone. Piles of shells, a common sight on many shores today, may one day form shelly limestones. In the deep oceans there is a constant 'rain' of the remains of tiny animals. About 100 million years ago there were lots of shallow seas in which small animals called coccoliths floated. Over millions of years their remains have built up huge thicknesses of chalk rock. Not surprisingly, limestones are among the best rocks in which to look for fossil shells, sea urchins, corals, sea lilies and many others.

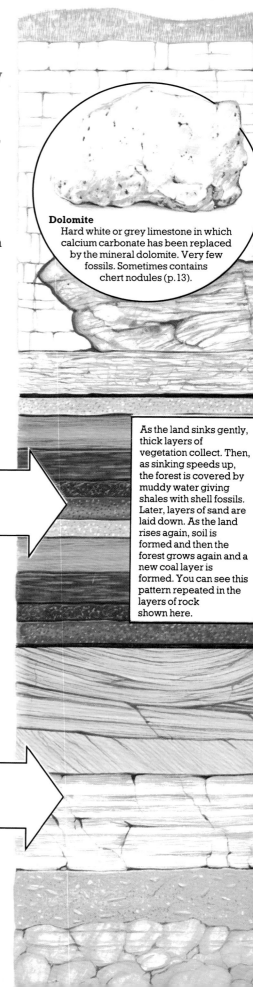

Dolomite
Hard white or grey limestone in which calcium carbonate has been replaced by the mineral dolomite. Very few fossils. Sometimes contains chert nodules (p.13).

How coal is formed

In the Carboniferous Period, about 300 million years ago, swamp forests covered much of North America, Asia and Europe. Great thicknesses of plant material became buried so quickly that they did not rot away completely. Instead they became compressed into rock consisting mainly of carbon. That rock is coal – one of our 'fossil fuels'. Sea level in the swamps kept changing, so the coal beds are often separated by beds of clay and sand.

As the land sinks gently, thick layers of vegetation collect. Then, as sinking speeds up, the forest is covered by muddy water giving shales with shell fossils. Later, layers of sand are laid down. As the land rises again, soil is formed and then the forest grows again and a new coal layer is formed. You can see this pattern repeated in the layers of rock shown here.

Sandstones

Sandstones may start off as beach or river sands or as desert sand dunes. After millions of years, new minerals grow between the grains and cement them into solid rock. Sand that has been rolled around for a long time gives sandstone with rounded grains; sand buried very quickly usually has sharp, angular grains.
    The Grand Canyon cuts through nearly 2,000 metres of mainly sandstone rocks.

Fossil limestones
Shelly limestones and reef limestones are often packed with fossils. Shells, corals and crinoids are cemented together in fine calcite rock.

Oolitic limestone
The tiny ooliths are about 1mm across and look like fish eggs. Larger ones (up to pea size) are called pisoliths. The cement is very fine calcite.

Chalk
Fine-grained white rock, usually quite soft. Made of pure calcite (a drop of vinegar makes it fizz). Often contains good fossils, and layers of flint nodules.

Coal
Shiny black rock, mainly carbon so it is dirty to handle. Sometimes contains leaf or stem prints. Fossils are more common in the clay and shale between seams.

Red sandstone
Many red sandstones formed in deserts. The quartz grains are well rounded, even highly polished. Desert sands often have sweeping curved bedding.

Sandstone (Grit)
This coarse grey sandstone was formed in a region of fast deposition. The grains were buried quickly and remain angular. Graded beds are common (see panel).

Shale
Very fine sediment (mud) hardens into mudstone. If the beds are very thin, the rock splits easily and is called shale. Fossils are quite common.

Calcite or quartz?

Sometimes it is hard to tell limestone from quartzite (p.14) just by looking. Here are two tests. You can scratch limestone with a knife – but not quartzite. A few drops of dilute hydrochloric acid will make limestone fizz: quartz does not. (Ordinary vinegar will make soft limestones and chalk fizz.)

From peat to coal

There are several stages in the formation of coal. See if you can collect samples of each. **Peat** is used in many countries as fuel. When dry, it is light and brown in colour. If you separate the material with tweezers you may find stems and seed cases from the original bog plants. **Lignite,** or 'brown coal', is the next stage. It is more compact than peat but you can still find bits of plant material. **Bituminous coal** is the familiar household coal and may contain plant fossils. **Anthracite** is the final stage. It is very hard, shiny and clean to handle, but contains no fossils.

Automatic sorting

Many sandstones have 'graded beds' and this experiment shows how grains of different sizes separate into different layers when deposited in water.

Fill a large jar about one-third full with garden soil, then top up with water. Stir well and leave it to settle. In a few days you will have 'graded bedding' in your jar.

1 Small stones
2 Grit
3 Silt
4 Fine mud
5 Very thin black layer of carbon from plant remains.

Pebbles and puddingstones

When pieces of rock are swept into a river they are dragged, pushed and rolled along until the corners are worn away. In the same way, the sea batters rock from cliffs, and then rolls the fragments around until they too become smooth and round.

Pebbles are simply water-worn fragments of rock. Just like specks of mud, coarse sand, and even large boulders, they can end up being cemented into rocks. When that happens, the rock is called a conglomerate, or a 'puddingstone'. Some of these are found among the earth's oldest rocks – so we know that water was present when they formed.

Search for interesting pebbles close to the water-line – the colours show up best when the pebbles are wet. Visit the beach after storms or high tides when the waves will have mixed everything up and brought new pebbles to the top.

You may find all the large pebbles at one end of the beach while the smaller ones have been carried to the other end by the waves.

Sorting your collection

The scientific way to group your pebbles is by rock type, but it is also interesting to sort them by shape. Very hard rocks like granite produce ball-shaped pebbles. Rocks that split into slabs (like many sedimentary and metamorphic rocks) produce discs. Quartzite sometimes produces cigar-shaped pebbles by constant rolling.

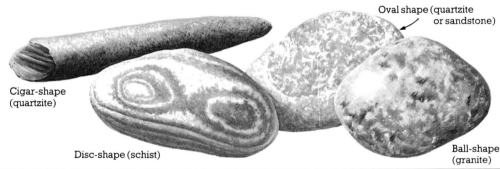

Oval shape (quartzite or sandstone)

Cigar-shape (quartzite)

Disc-shape (schist)

Ball-shape (granite)

Polishing pebbles

Very hard pebbles with good colours can be polished in a tumbler. The best pebbles are the various kinds of quartz (agate, amethyst, jasper and rock crystal) but softer pebbles like limestone, marble, jet and amber also polish well. The drum of the tumbler is three-quarters filled with small pebbles, then water and grinding powder are added. The pebbles are tumbled for several days to smooth and polish them (see page 32.)

Cracked and pitted pebbles will not polish well so throw them out.

Each stage of tumbling and polishing may take several days.

Natural pebbles can be displayed in a water tank to show off their colours. You can also varnish them, paint them, or use their shapes to make models.

This is what some common pebbles look like before and after polishing.

Green quartz

Amethyst

Red jasper

You can buy simple jewellery fittings and turn your best stones into rings, cuff-links, brooches and necklaces.

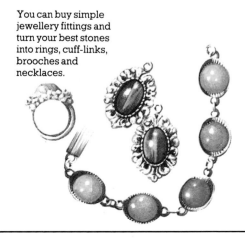

Pebbles past and present

Rock fragments carried along by the glacier help to gouge its typical U-shaped valley (1). Later the debris is dumped as layers of boulder clay or 'till' (2). The granite boulder (3) was carried by a glacier and left stranded on a hillside.

①

② Boulder clay (moraine)

③ 'Perched' boulder

The middle section of a river (1) is fast and powerful and is able to carry a lot of rock fragments. Pebbles may be swirled round in one place for so long that they wear a pothole (2). Pebbles stacked against each other in a rock layer (3) show the current direction in an ancient river.

①

②

③ Current flow →

Waves (1) usually sweep pebbles up the beach at an angle. But when the water rushes back, the pebbles also roll straight back down the slope. That way the pebbles zigzag along the shore (2) – sometimes for long distances. The pebbles of ancient beaches can be seen in conglomerates (3).

①

② In, In, Out, Out

③

Rocks within rocks

In some sedimentary rocks, such as chalk, sandstone and shale, you may find lumps which separate easily from the rest of the rock. They are usually spherical or bun-shaped although all kinds of strange shapes occur. If the lump is of a *different* material from the surrounding rock it is called a **nodule.** Flint is the most common.

If the lump you find is made of the *same* material as the surrounding rock, it is called a **concretion.** The lump is hard because the rock has been cemented together by another mineral – often calcite or silica. Among the most beautiful concretions are 'desert roses' formed when gypsum or baryte cements grains of sand together.

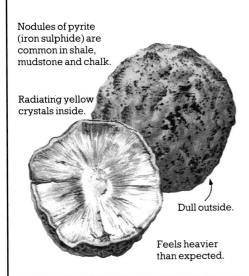

Nodules of pyrite (iron sulphide) are common in shale, mudstone and chalk.

Radiating yellow crystals inside.

Dull outside.

Feels heavier than expected.

Flint nodules are chalky white outside: smooth and black inside.

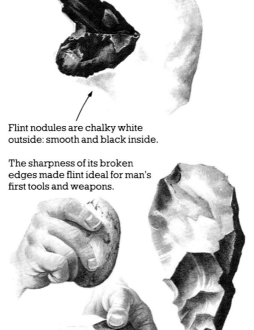

The sharpness of its broken edges made flint ideal for man's first tools and weapons.

Disc-shaped mudstone concretions form parallel to the layers of rock.

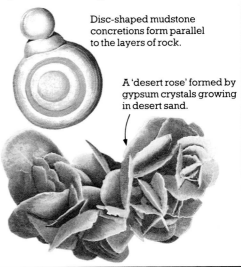

A 'desert rose' formed by gypsum crystals growing in desert sand.

New rocks for old

Rocks that have been changed by high temperatures and great pressures are called metamorphic rocks. They may have started off as sedimentary rocks, or igneous rocks, or even as older metamorphic rocks being changed for a second time. When they are heated, or squeezed by movements deep inside the earth's crust, new minerals grow inside the rocks. Geologists estimate how much a rock has been altered by studying the new minerals that have formed.
'Contact metamorphism' occurs when rocks are changed by heat alone – usually when hot igneous rocks are intruded, for example as sills and dykes. What kind of new rock is formed depends on what the original rock was made of.

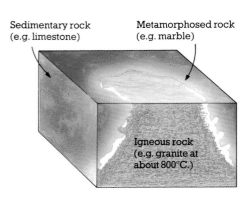

Sedimentary rock (e.g. limestone) Metamorphosed rock (e.g. marble)

Igneous rock (e.g. granite at about 800°C.)

Skarn
New rock formed when iron, magnesium and silica from the magma mix with the calcite and other minerals in the limestone. Often contains crystals of garnet, olivine and pyroxene.

Marble
White or grey but often contains pale streaks of colour. Mainly calcite but may also contain dolomite. Often looks very like quartzite – but marble scratches easily with a knife.

Spotted shale
Fine-grained dark grey, green or purple rock that splits into thin sheets. Often has dark oval or round spots on fresh surfaces. May also have rectangular andalusite crystals.

Hornfels
Closer to the intrusion, the shale merges into darker, finer-grained hornfels. Shiny mica flakes may be visible with a lens. Long thin crystals with black centres are chiastolite.

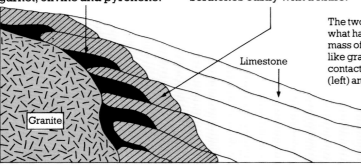

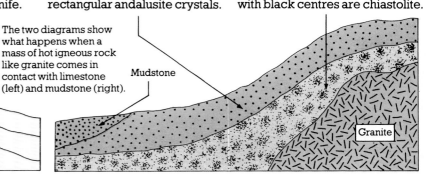

Limestone

Granite

The two diagrams show what happens when a mass of hot igneous rock like granite comes in contact with limestone (left) and mudstone (right).

Mudstone

Granite

Mountain-building rocks

When two of the 'rafts' of the earth's crust collide, all the sediments in between are crushed, folded, and squeezed up into a new mountain chain. New rocks are formed by the pressure, *and* by heat from the mantle below. This is called 'regional metamorphism'.

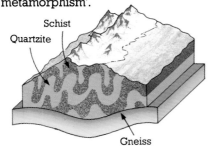

Schist
Quartzite
Gneiss

Quartzite   Schist   Gneiss

Quartzite is metamorphosed sandstone. Like the original sand, it is made almost entirely of quartz, but this is recrystallized into a mass of interlocking quartz crystals in place of the original separate grains. **Schists** are formed when sedimentary rocks grow new flaky minerals such as mica and chlorite. Like slates, they split easily in one direction. Some contain good garnet crystals. **Gneiss** is a finely banded rock formed in the middle of the fold belt where temperatures are very high.

Rocks formed by squeezing

Some metamorphic rocks are formed by very high pressure, without any heat at all. If sedimentary rocks such as shales are squeezed, for example when rocks are being folded, tiny flakes of mica recrystallize at right-angles to the pressure. The result is that the rock splits easily in this direction. It has been turned into slate, and is said to have good 'cleavage'. Most slates form from shales and mudstones but volcanic tuffs may also be altered into slates. Often the bedding planes can still be seen in the rock. Slate is very useful for covering roofs, and because it is very hard and flat it is used for billiard table tops.

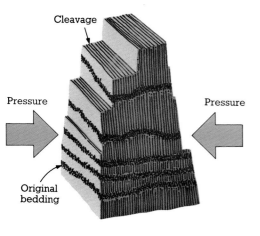

Cleavage

Pressure

Pressure

Original bedding

Coarser slate with crystals of iron pyrites in tiny cubes.

Fine-grained 'roofing' slate

The huge quarries of North Wales are famous for their finely cleaved roofing slates. Most quarries are in rock of Cambrian, Ordovician and Silurian age (see pages 24-25).

Things to look for

Where rocks have been squeezed and folded, the minerals in them, and any pebbles and fossils they contain, will often be crushed out of shape.

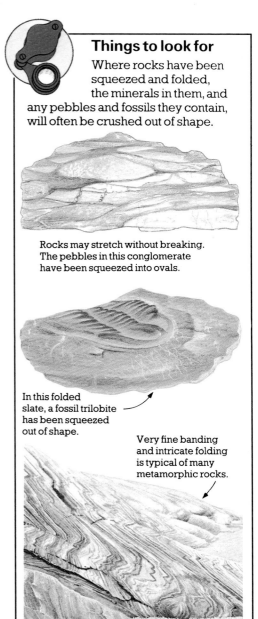

Rocks may stretch without breaking. The pebbles in this conglomerate have been squeezed into ovals.

In this folded slate, a fossil trilobite has been squeezed out of shape.

Very fine banding and intricate folding is typical of many metamorphic rocks.

Experiments with folds

The diagram at the right shows how folds may vary from simple up and down folds called upright anticlines and synclines, to huge overfolds with faults cutting through them.

Anticline

Syncline

Overfold

Faulted fold

Thrust-faulted fold

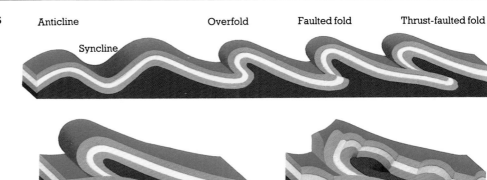

Build up several layers of coloured plasticine or modelling clay and push them into a simple fold.

Keep pushing until the fold overturns and the layers in the middle begin to tear.

Finally use a spoon to 'carve' a mountain. Now you can see why rock layers make such complex patterns on geology maps.

Understanding minerals

Man has been using minerals in his everyday life ever since he discovered that a sharp-edged piece of flint made an excellent tool or weapon. Today, minerals provide all our metals. They are the raw materials for fertilizers. and the chemical industry. And they are used in making paper, paint, soft drinks and medicines – everything, in fact, from school chalk and aircraft to hamburgers and video tapes.

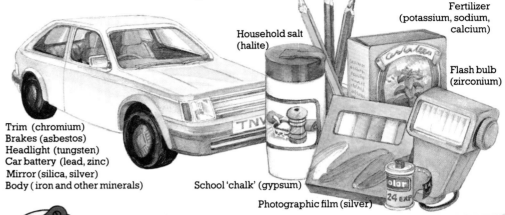

Aircraft (aluminium, carbon)

Minerals around us

'Lead' pencil (graphite)

Fertilizer (potassium, sodium, calcium)

Household salt (halite)

Flash bulb (zirconium)

Trim (chromium)
Brakes (asbestos)
Headlight (tungsten)
Car battery (lead, zinc)
Mirror (silica, silver)
Body (iron and other minerals)

School 'chalk' (gypsum)

Photographic film (silver)

Mineral or rock – What's the difference?

Minerals are the building blocks from which rocks are made. Some minerals, such as gold, sulphur and copper, consist entirely of one chemical element. These are called 'native elements'. Other minerals are more complicated mixtures of elements. An important property of minerals is that their composition is always the same. Quartz, for example, always consists of one-third silicon and two-thirds oxygen. The salt we use on our food always has one atom of sodium to each one of chlorine. The examples below show how minerals are built up of elements.

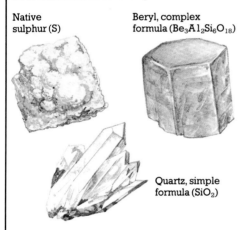

Native sulphur (S)

Beryl, complex formula $(Be_3Al_2Si_6O_{18})$

Quartz, simple formula (SiO_2)

Rocks, on the other hand, are nearly always mixtures of minerals – and because they are formed in different ways (and may even be changed after they are formed) their 'recipes' can vary quite a lot. Granite is usually about 20% quartz, 75% feldspar and 5% mica, but the proportions vary and the rock often contains small amounts of other minerals as well. The rocks below are all granites.

How to identify minerals

Minerals can be identified by their colour, hardness and density, and by the characteristic shapes they have. Try these tests on some common minerals and then compare your results with the mineral descriptions on the following pages.

Streak is the colour of the mineral in powder form (often quite different from its normal colour). Test by scraping your sample across the unglazed back of an ordinary household tile.

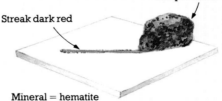

Sample black

Streak dark red

Mineral = hematite

Magnetism provides an immediate clue to the mineral magnetite. Pins and paper clips cling to the sample.

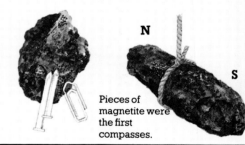

N

S

Pieces of magnetite were the first compasses.

Hardness is one of the most useful tests. The scale goes from talc (1), the softest mineral, to diamond (10) the hardest. You can buy sets of 1 to 9 in mineral shops. Each test piece will scratch minerals that are softer but will be scratched by those that are harder. Some everyday objects can be used to give a rough guide to a mineral's hardness.

Minerals of hardness 6 or more will scratch glass.

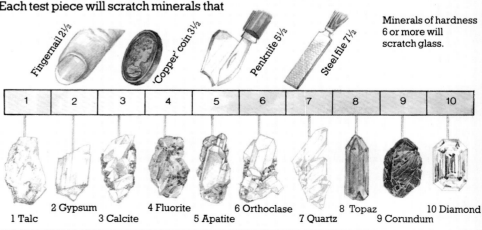

Fingernail 2½   'Copper' coin 3½   Penknife 5½   Steel file 7½

1	2	3	4	5	6	7	8	9	10

1 Talc
2 Gypsum
3 Calcite
4 Fluorite
5 Apatite
6 Orthoclase
7 Quartz
8 Topaz
9 Corundum
10 Diamond

Riches below ground

Minerals can become concentrated into useful deposits in several ways. Some ores crystallize directly out of magmas. Others form when minerals crystallize out of hot water solutions deep inside the earth. Some deposits, like coal seams and salt beds, simply build up where they are formed. Others, especially heavy minerals like gold, may be weathered out of their original rocks and carried many miles before being dumped in river or beach gravels. Oil seeps up through the tiny spaces in rocks until it is trapped by a non-porous layer.

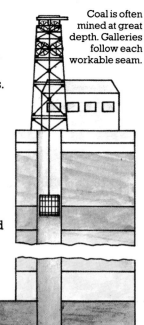

Coal is often mined at great depth. Galleries follow each workable seam.

Copper and iron ores are often worked in huge open-cast mines.

High pressure water jets are used to quarry the soft clay mineral kaolinite ('China clay').

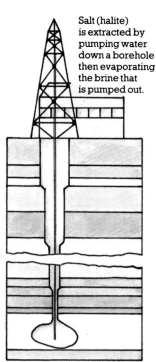

Salt (halite) is extracted by pumping water down a borehole then evaporating the brine that is pumped out.

Cleavage planes are the surfaces along which a mineral breaks. The number of cleavage planes a mineral has, and the angles between them, provide useful clues to identification. (See p.21 for measuring angles.)

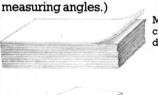

Mica has perfect cleavage in one direction only.

Feldspar has two cleavage directions. This gives four smooth surfaces and two rough ones.

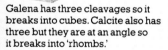

Galena has three cleavages so it breaks into cubes. Calcite also has three but they are at an angle so it breaks into 'rhombs.'

Fluorite and diamond are examples of minerals with four cleavages. They form double-pyramid crystals.

Shape, also called 'habit', can be a useful clue to minerals that do not form large flat-sided crystals. These examples are shapes made up of thousands of tiny crystals. Each habit has a special name.

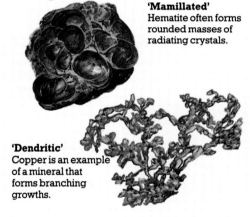

'Mamillated'
Hematite often forms rounded masses of radiating crystals.

'Dendritic'
Copper is an example of a mineral that forms branching growths.

'Fibrous'
Asbestos forms masses of long thin parallel crystals that 'fray' into mineral 'wool'.

Density is another very important property. You can measure it with this simple home-made apparatus.

Hang your specimen from the long arm of the balance and add weights (bulldog clips are ideal) to the other arm. Adjust the position of the specimen backward or forward on the arm until it is balanced and the pointer is *exactly* opposite the reference mark. Note the number of scale units at the point where the sample is hanging. Call this reading A. Now place a container of water under the sample so that it is submerged. Don't move the bulldog counterweights at all. Instead, slide your sample along to its new balance point. Take a new reading B.
The density of your sample is given by this simple formula:

$$\text{Density} = B \div (B - A)$$

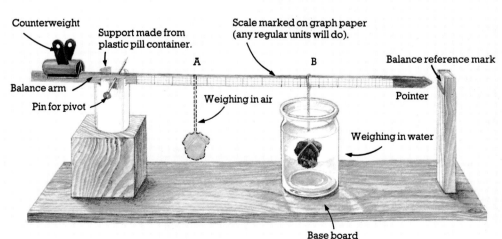

Counterweight

Support made from plastic pill container.

Scale marked on graph paper (any regular units will do).

Balance reference mark

Balance arm

Pin for pivot

A

B

Weighing in air

Pointer

Weighing in water

Base board

So, if your first reading had been 8 units and the second 12 units, the density would have been 12/12-8 = 3.

Minerals to look for

A really good mineral collection makes a spectacular display and is especially satisfying when you can point to each specimen and remember where and when you found it. However, some minerals are more difficult to find than others, and some are quite rare in certain countries, so you may want to add to your collection by occasionally buying a specimen of a particularly interesting mineral from one of the many specialized shops.

The silica family

Quartz is made of silicon and oxygen and is one of the most common rock-forming minerals. It usually occurs as grains and small crystals but well-formed crystals are often found in veins and geodes (p.9). Streak is colourless. Hardness 7. Density 2.6.

Quartz in large crystals

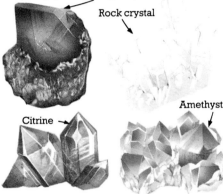

Smoky quartz (cairngorm)

Rock crystal

Citrine

Amethyst

Quartz in masses of minute crystals

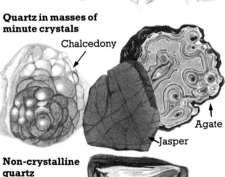

Chalcedony

Agate

Jasper

Non-crystalline quartz

Opal

Tourmaline is one of the minerals you may find in pegmatites (p.8). It usually forms long crystals with ridges along the sides. The cross-section is triangular, with slightly curved sides. Usually black but occasionally blue, pink or green ones are found. Streak white. Hardness 7½. Density 3.2.

Mica may be dark brown (called biotite) or silvery white (called muscovite). Forms characteristic stacks or 'books' of thin flakes that can be separated with a pin or knife blade. Both kinds are common in granite and pegmatite (p.8) and in schists (p.14).

Baryte is usually white and often slightly transparent. It may also be brown or pink and often forms good crystals. Found in veins in limestone. Contains the element barium which gives the bright green colour in flares and fireworks. Streak white. Hardness 2½-3½. Density 4.3-4.6.

Calcite forms more different crystal shapes than any other mineral. When broken it always forms six-sided fragments called 'rhombs' (p.21). Usually white but may be grey, green, yellow, reddish or even blue. Streak is white. Hardness 3. Density 2.7. Calcite forms stalactites and stalagmites in limestone caves.

Fluorite, or fluorspar, comes in a wide range of colours but blue, green, purple and yellow are the most common. Streak white. Hardness 4. Density 3.2. Ultra-violet light makes the mineral glow – an effect that is called fluorescence, after the mineral.

Malachite is a carbonate of copper. A very attractive mineral – often with bands of colour in circular patterns. Like calcite it will fizz in dilute hydrochloric acid. It is an important copper ore and is used as a decorative stone.

Galena is made of the elements lead and sulphur and is one of the main ores of lead. When broken it splits easily into small cube-shaped pieces. The mineral is shiny when broken but soon becomes dull grey. Streak grey. Hardness only 2½. But very heavy – density 7.5. Usually found in veins in limestone.

Gypsum may form clear crystals (selenite) or white fibrous masses across veins (satin spar). There is also a fine-grained white variety called alabaster, used for carving. Hardness only 2 (it will scratch with a fingernail). Streak white. Density 2.3. Gypsum is mined to make plaster, cement, coated paper and paints.

Magnetite is one of the ores of iron. It is sometimes found as diamond-shaped crystals but more usually forms irregular lumps. Colour and streak black. Hardness 5½-6½. Density 5.2. It is strongly magnetic (p.16).

Feldspars are the most common rock-forming minerals. There are two main types – orthoclase, rich in potassium, and plagioclase, rich in sodium and calcium. Orthoclase is the milky white or pink mineral in granite. Hardness 6-6½. Density 2.5-2.6. Labradorite, one of the plagioclase feldspars, often shows spectacular blues and greens.

Chalcopyrite, or copper pyrites, is made of copper, iron and sulphur. It is bright yellow when fresh but tarnishes to a rainbow of colours. Because of its appearance it is also called 'fool's gold'. Streak greenish black. Hardness 3½-4. Density 4.1-4.3.

Pyrite, or iron pyrites, is made of iron and sulphur. It usually forms good crystals, especially small cubes with parallel lines on the faces. Also forms nodules (p.13). Pale brassy yellow colour with greenish-black streak. Hardness 6-6½. Density 4.9-5.2.

Panning for gold

Because gold is so heavy (density 19.3) its tiny grains and nuggets tend to collect in river sands and gravels when the original rock is weathered away. The prospector can separate the gold by swirling river sand in a shallow pan so that lighter particles are washed over the side. The heavy gold stays at the bottom.

The silt in the pan often contains particles of heavy black iron minerals as well as gold and these are separated out with a magnet once the silt has been allowed to dry.

Hematite is the most important iron ore. It often forms smooth kidney-shaped masses and may be dull grey, black or dark red in colour. Common in sedimentary rocks where it may also form ooliths (p.10). Also forms shiny metallic-grey crystals. Streak red. Hardness 5-6. Density 4.9-5.3.

19

Crystals and gemstones

Minerals are made of atoms of different elements such as oxygen, silicon, carbon, lead and so on. The atoms are packed together in simple patterns and the pattern is always the same in any particular mineral. It is these hidden patterns that give mineral crystals their characteristic shapes. Minerals only form good crystals when they have room to grow freely – in a molten mass of igneous rock, for example, or in a cavity in a rock. That is why the best crystals are often found in geodes, which are spaces in the rock caused by trapped bubbles of gas or pockets of liquid. Perfect crystals are hard to find, but even when they have grown slightly lop-sided, the angles will always be the same.

Two-faced carbon

The carbon atoms in diamond are locked together by chemical bonds in three directions. This makes the mineral very hard and is why it is used for cutters, drills and bits in industry. When atoms of carbon are joined in just two directions, as in graphite, the mineral forms thin plates that slide easily over each other. This is why graphite feels slippery and is widely used as an industrial lubricant.

Crystal showers

You can explore the amazing variety of crystal shapes by looking at snowflakes. Catch them on a piece of black card or cloth that has been kept cold in a refrigerator. Look at them with your lens – you will never find two exactly the same!

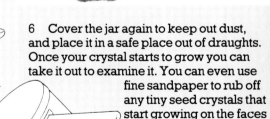

A large group of natural amethyst crystals.

How to grow crystals

You can grow your own crystals quite easily, either from a ready-made kit or by buying some white or chrome *alum* from a chemist and following these simple instructions. But remember to treat chemicals with care. Wash your hands thoroughly and be sure to wash all containers when you have finished. Growing crystals is a good way of learning about how minerals behave in solutions, and how crystals grow.

1. Dissolve four or five ounces of alum in a pint of water and heat it (without boiling). *Add more alum until no more will dissolve.* This gives what is called a 'saturated solution'.

2. Take the pan off the heat and pour a little liquid into a saucer. This will provide your 'seed' crystals so put it in a safe place. (A cool cupboard is ideal.)

3. Pour the rest of the solution into a clean glass jar and cover it with a cloth to keep out dust.

4. In a few days, small crystals will appear in the saucer. Leave them until they are 2-3mm across, then pour off the liquid and dry them on a piece of tissue.

5. Pour your main solution into a clean jar, leaving behind any small crystals that may have formed. Then hang your best seed crystal in the solution using thread and a simple wire frame. Make sure that all the wire is under the surface.

6. Cover the jar again to keep out dust, and place it in a safe place out of draughts. Once your crystal starts to grow you can take it out to examine it. You can even use fine sandpaper to rub off any tiny seed crystals that start growing on the faces of the main crystal.

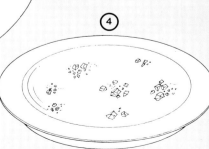

Carbon:1
Tiny industrial diamonds give this rock-cutter its tough cutting edge.

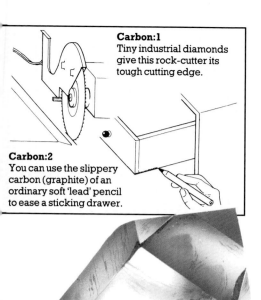

Carbon:2
You can use the slippery carbon (graphite) of an ordinary soft 'lead' pencil to ease a sticking drawer.

Gemstones

To be classed as a gemstone a mineral must be rare, beautiful and very hard (so that it will not scratch).

Diamonds are found only in pipe-like intrusions that come from deep inside the earth. The rock is called kimberlite after the famous Kimberley diamond mine in South Africa.

Emerald is a variety of the mineral beryl, which usually forms pale green six-sided crystals. The very rare deep green transparent stones come mainly from South America.

Sapphire and ruby are varieties of the mineral corundum which is usually yellow, brown or green. When it is a rich transparent blue it is called sapphire. The very rare blood-red stone is called ruby.

Semi-precious stones are less rare, and, because they are softer, not as long-lasting. They include many varieties of quartz (panel on p.18), jet (fossilized wood), amber (fossil tree resin) and many other minerals.

Rough diamond in kimberlite

The world's largest cut diamond – the 'Star of Africa No. 1' in the Royal Sceptre.

Cut emerald

Cut ruby

Star sapphire showing its characteristic star of reflected light.

Semi-precious stones

Wood opal (fossil wood replaced by silica).

Amber containing an insect trapped when sticky resin oozed from a tree.

Chinese jade buckles are made from the minerals jadeite and nephrite.

These large alum crystals have been allowed to grow into each other. Notice how all the angles are the same, even though some of the faces are not complete.

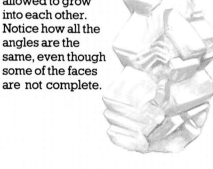

Crystal twins

Many minerals form 'twins' when two or more crystals grow together. Look out for twins whenever you find well-formed crystals. They are very common in feldspars.

'Swallow-tail' twins in gypsum.

Seeing double

Calcite splits easily into flat rectangular pieces. If you place one of these over an object, you will see a double image due to the unusual way the mineral causes the rays of light to bend.

7   When the crystal stops growing you can dry it on tissue and store it in a padded matchbox. To make it bigger, make up a new batch of solution and hang the crystal in it. (The solution *must* be saturated – otherwise it will dissolve your crystal instead of making it grow!)

To measure the angles between the faces of your crystals, mark out the shape of a 180 degree protractor on stiff card. Cut it out and mark on the divisions. Add a pointer of card, using a split-pin fastener so that it can swing round. Place your crystal against the two edges as shown and read off the angle.

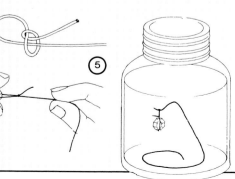

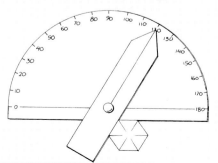

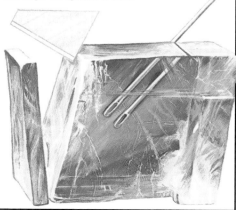

All about fossils

Every animal and plant that dies on earth could be fossilized – but it has to die in the right place. If its body is eaten, or rots away, or is broken up by the sea, it is lost for ever. But if it is buried quickly by mud or sand, there is a good chance that it will be fossilized. The most likely place for quick burial is in the sea where sediments are collecting all the time. That is why most fossils are found in marine sediments. It also explains why shells, sea urchins and corals are common fossils while land animals like birds, monkeys, dinosaurs and insects are much rarer.

Fortunately for palaeontologists (people who study fossils) there are other places where fossils can form. Lakes, ponds, lagoons and estuaries often contain remains of plants, fishes and small animals. Natural tar pits sometimes contain perfect fossils. And mammoths have been found in the frozen earth of the Arctic, with even the hair and skin preserved.

How fossils are made

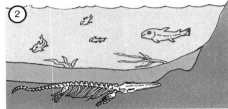

Millions of years ago an Ichthyosaur (1) died and sank to the seabed. The soft body decayed but the skeleton was buried by sediments (2). Very slowly the bones were replaced by other minerals to form a perfect fossil (3). This was later brought to the surface by earth movements and uncovered (4) by erosion.

The illustrations below show some of the different types of fossils you are likely to come across.

Growth rings can sometimes be seen on the trees.

Minerals dissolved in water seeping through the rocks have replaced the original wood of these ancient trees.

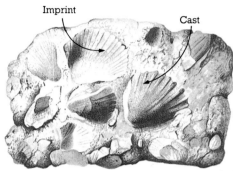

Imprint

Cast

Shelly limestones often contain 'imprints' of the outside surfaces of shells and 'casts' of the insides.

Collecting and cleaning fossils

Before hammering, take a close look at the rock. Use its natural lines of weakness. This collector is tapping a piece of rock so that it will break along the bedding plane (horizontal) and the diamond-shaped pattern of 'joints'. He is steadying the rock so that it does not fall and damage the fossil he has found.

Many good fossils are broken when collectors try to trim them on the spot. Be patient. Take them home where you can work carefully with the fossil securely clamped, as shown here, or firmly bedded down on a canvas bag filled with sand. This preparation board is easy to make and simply hooks on to the edge of a table or workbench.

Wrap each specimen in newspaper with the thickest part of the wrapping covering the fossil.

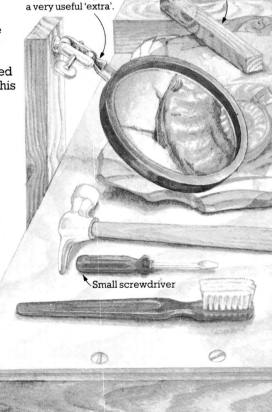

A mounted magnifier is a very useful 'extra'.

Adjustable clamp

Small screwdriver

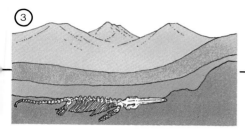

Occasionally you may be lucky and find a shell fossil with some of the original shell covering the surface.

Leaf fossils are very delicate imprints and must be treated with great care.

Fossil tracks and signs

Sometimes the animal itself is not preserved – but its tracks are. These are called 'trace fossils'. Dinosaur footprints have been found in several countries – and even the footprints of man's

This 150-million-year-old king crab was fossilized along with the track of its last seabed walk.

Dinosaur footprints sometimes show amazing detail of the animal's skin, and the deep imprints of its claws.

ancestors have been found in one-million-year-old rocks in Africa. Worm burrows, trilobite tracks, and even the marks of raindrops and the cracks in dried-up mud may be preserved.

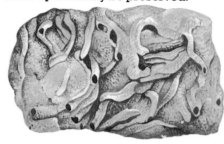

These perfectly preserved 'cement' tubes were made by tiny worms living on the bed of a shallow sea.

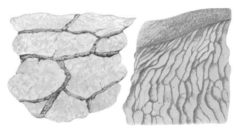

Mud cracks and beach ripple marks are often fossilized in mudstones and beds of sandstone.

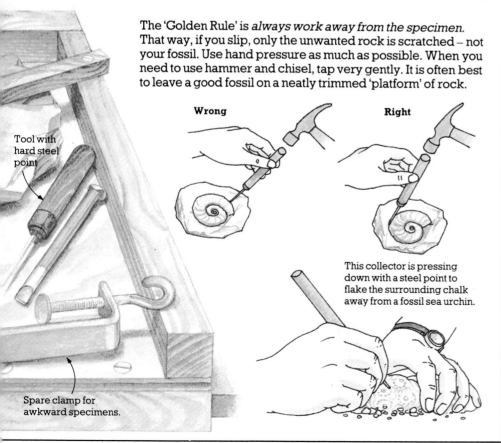

Tool with hard steel point

Spare clamp for awkward specimens.

The 'Golden Rule' is *always work away from the specimen.* That way, if you slip, only the unwanted rock is scratched – not your fossil. Use hand pressure as much as possible. When you need to use hammer and chisel, tap very gently. It is often best to leave a good fossil on a neatly trimmed 'platform' of rock.

Wrong　　　　　**Right**

This collector is pressing down with a steel point to flake the surrounding chalk away from a fossil sea urchin.

Making fossil casts

Many modelling shops sell rubber late: moulding kits. Build up several layers over your fossil, allowing each to dry thoroughly. Then slit the back of the mould and peel it off the fossil. You can then use the mould to make plaster of paris casts of the original fossil. These can be painted and varnished for display or made into gifts.

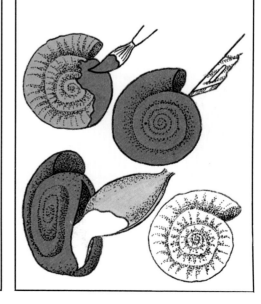

The story fossils tell

In the 16th century a man called James Ussher calculated that the earth was created in 4,004BC. Today we believe that it happened closer to 4,600 *million* years ago. The story has been unfolded by studying the rocks themselves and the fossils they contain. The first signs of life are found in rocks nearly 3,500 million years old, but these were very simple one-celled plants called algae. For several thousand million years, very little happened. Then, about 600 million years ago, life really 'took off'. Shells, and later back-bones, evolved and more and more complex animals began to appear. Since then, thousands of plants and animals have evolved, reigned for a while, then become extinct. But all have left their mark. Who knows what new forms of life may roam the earth fifty million years from now?

Man – the newcomer

In some ways the dinosaurs could be called the most successful group of all time. After all, they ruled the earth for 140 million years. But no other animal has ever evolved as far, or as quickly, as man. Just one and a half million years ago the first true men stood upright, yet today man dominates the earth and is using advanced technology to explore deep into space.

'Upright man' (*Homo erectus*) appeared in Asia and Africa 1½ m.y.ago. He used simple tools of wood and stone.

10,000 years ago, Stone Age men kept sheep and goats and grew wheat and barley for food.

'Thinking man' (*Homo sapiens*)

The Palaeozoic Era

The name means 'The era of ancient life'. Most of the invertebrates (animals without backbones) evolved and were soon followed by animals with bony skeletons. Amphibians evolved from fishes and moved on to the land about half way through the era. These in turn gave way to the reptiles. The first complex plants appeared on land about 420 million years ago. At the end of the era Antarctica, Africa, India and South America were grouped near the South Pole (see pages 6-7).

The Mesozoic Era

In the 'middle life' era the dinosaurs ruled the land, and sea reptiles ruled the oceans. This was the Age of the Reptiles'. The climate was generally warm, and the continents we know today were formed by the break-up of the huge ancient 'supercontinent' Gondwanaland (p.6). They were still, however, very far from their present positions. The end of the era was marked by world-wide extinction of the giant reptiles, all the belemnites, and all but one of the ammonite group. The survivor, still living, was *Nautilus* (p.27).

The Cenozoic Era

The 'new life' era saw the mammals quickly take over from the reptiles as rulers of the land. Many huge and strange-looking mammals evolved but soon became extinct, leaving the stage free for the ancestors of our modern deer, antelopes, elephants, bats, kangaroos, mice and countless others. The flowering plants evolved and clothed the land with trees and grasses, and there was a huge increase in the numbers of insects. Man evolved from his forest-ape ancestors about four million years ago to begin the most incredible 'success story' in the three and a half million year story of life on earth.

570
40

CAMBRIAN PERIOD
Abundant trilobites and shelled animals.

530
90

ORDOVICIAN PERIOD
First corals; graptolites and shelled animals common.

4

SILURIAN PERIOD
Armoured fish appear.

DEVONIAN PERIOD
Bony fishes abundant; first amphibians and first (wingless) insects

CARBONIFEROUS PERIOD
Increase of reptiles, amphibians and sharks. Flying insects appear

CRETACEOUS PERIOD
The end of the 'Age of Reptiles' – all the dinosaurs extinct. Huge increase in plant life and insects; many new (small) mammals.

PALAEOCENE AND EOCENE
Mammals begin to dominate the land, including the ancestors of modern mammals. First snakes appear. Many new shellfish appear in the seas.

OLIGOCENE
More modern-type mammals appear, including elephants, deer and horses, plus ancestors of dogs, cats and bears.

MIOCENE
Plant life very like today, with beech, poplar, oak and many other trees. Mammal life included many apes, and the primitive ancestors of man.

PLIOCENE 'Man-apes' and the first tool- using primitive men appear.

PLEISTOCENE Man stands upright.

The 4,000 million years between the formation of the earth and the start of the detailed fossil record is called the Precambrian Period.

The oldest rocks so far dated are about 3,780 million years ol

4,000 m.y.ago

4,600 million years ago

Life accelerates, with many soft-bodied animals like worms appearing.

1,400 m.y.ago, more complex types of algae began to appear.

About 1,500 m.y.ago, oxygen started to build up in the earth's atmosphere.

All figures are in millions of years

| How long ago it started |
| How long it lasted |

The Devonian world ▶

Horsetails, club mosses and ferns clothed the land. Amphibians like *Ichthyostega* (1) moved between land and water. The seas contained armoured fish including *Antiarchus* (2), *Drepanaspis* (3) and *Pteraspis* (4).

345 / 65

280 / 55

225 / 35

PERMIAN PERIOD
Many ancient species became extinct, including trilobites. Many new reptiles appear.

TRIASSIC PERIOD
Ammonites abundant. First dinosaurs and marine reptiles appear; also primitive mammals.

190 / 55

JURASSIC PERIOD
Dinosaurs rule the land and take to the air (pterosaurs). The first true bird evolves from reptilian ancestors.

135 / 71

The Jurassic world ▶

Dinosaurs included *Stegosaurus* (1) and *Diplodocus* (2). The first crocodiles appeared (3). *Rhamphorhynchus* (4) and the first bird *Archaeopteryx* (5) ruled the skies.

64 / 26

The Oligocene world ▶

The modern-looking landscape was home to *Brontotherium* (1), *Arsinoitherium* (2), *Moetherium* (3), *Hyrachus,* (4) and the hunter/scavenger *Andrewsarchus* (5).

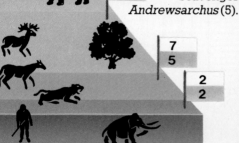

38 / 12

26 / 19

7 / 5

2 / 2

The first signs of life (very simple algae) appeared about 3,400 m.y.ago.

2,000 m.y.ago

2,500 m.y.ago

Identifying your fossils

The first step in identifying a fossil is to place it in one of the main animal or plant groups. Some of the main animal groups are shown here along with tips on what to look for. The next stage is to try and find the fossil in one of the more specialized books you will find in your library. You will usually find a close match – even if not the exact species. Finally you can compare your specimen with those on display in a museum, where you can also ask for advice.

Corals

The walls and partitions in corals are built up by tiny soft-bodied animals living one inside each compartment. Some corals are solitary, but most live in huge colonies that form coral reefs.

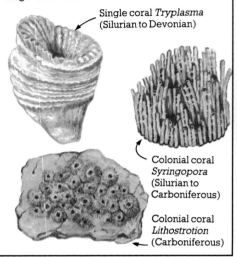

Single coral *Tryplasma* (Silurian to Devonian)

Colonial coral *Syringopora* (Silurian to Carboniferous)

Colonial coral *Lithostrotion* (Carboniferous)

Lampshells (Brachiopods)

These sea creatures have two shells (called 'valves') and one is usually bigger than the other. This gives some shells their characteristic 'oil lamp' shape. The shells may be smooth or have growth lines which follow the shell's outline. Some also have ridges and grooves that radiate out from the middle of the hinge. Brachiopods are common in rocks of Cambrian to Carboniferous age.

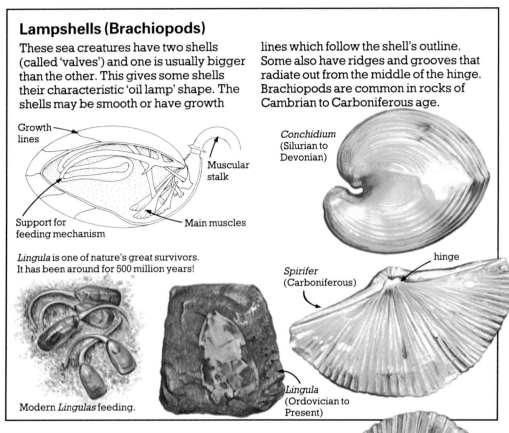

Growth lines

Muscular stalk

Support for feeding mechanism

Main muscles

Lingula is one of nature's great survivors. It has been around for 500 million years!

Modern *Lingulas* feeding.

Conchidium (Silurian to Devonian)

Spirifer (Carboniferous)

hinge

Lingula (Ordovician to Present)

Cockles and mussels (Bivalves)

Like brachiopods, the bivalves have two shells but they are both the same size and shape – even though the overall shape can vary a lot. The shells often show growth lines, and radiating ridges and grooves, useful for identification.

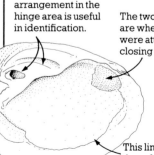

The tooth and socket arrangement in the hinge area is useful in identification.

The two oval patches are where the muscles were attached for closing the shell.

This line shows where the soft body of the shellfish was attached to the shell.

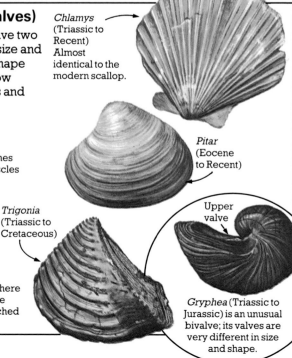

Chlamys (Triassic to Recent) Almost identical to the modern scallop.

Pitar (Eocene to Recent)

Trigonia (Triassic to Cretaceous)

Upper valve

Gryphea (Triassic to Jurassic) is an unusual bivalve; its valves are very different in size and shape.

Graptolites

These tiny sea creatures lived in little cups joined into strings. Some were fixed to rocks, but most simply drifted with the currents. They are usually found in shales and slates of Cambrian to Carboniferous age.

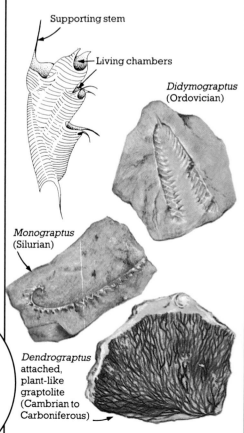

Supporting stem

Living chambers

Didymograptus (Ordovician)

Monograptus (Silurian)

Dendrograptus attached, plant-like graptolite (Cambrian to Carboniferous)

Trilobites

These extinct creatures were widespread in the sea from Cambrian to Permian times – for about 350 million years. They had head, body and tail sections, and the segmented body could roll up like an armadillo. They could swim, and also walk on the seabed. Trilobites are found mainly in mudstones and shales of Cambrian to Silurian age.

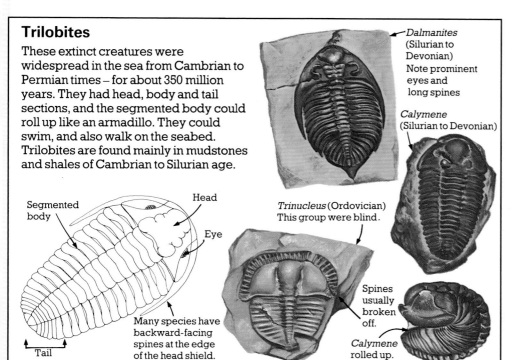

Dalmanites (Silurian to Devonian) Note prominent eyes and long spines

Calymene (Silurian to Devonian)

Trinucleus (Ordovician) This group were blind.

Spines usually broken off.

Calymene rolled up.

Segmented body

Head

Eye

Many species have backward-facing spines at the edge of the head shield.

Tail

Snails (Gastropods)

Most gastropods have coiled shells, either flat, like a wheel, or spiral, like a garden snail. The animal starts with a tiny shell and widens the main living chamber as it grows in a spiral round the central column.

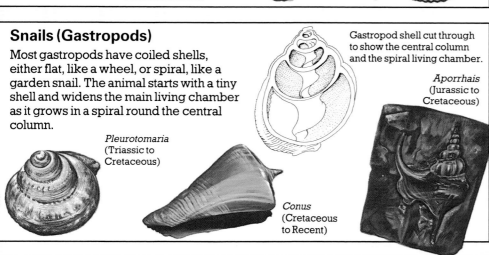

Gastropod shell cut through to show the central column and the spiral living chamber.

Aporrhais (Jurassic to Cretaceous)

Pleurotomaria (Triassic to Cretaceous)

Conus (Cretaceous to Recent)

Sea urchins and sea lilies (Echinoderms)

Sea urchins are round or heart-shaped animals with a shell (really an external skeleton) made of calcite. They are covered with knobs of various sizes and patterns and in life these carried spines.

The spines are usually missing in fossils but you can see them on modern urchins in rock pools. Sea lilies (crinoids) are found in limestones from Ordovician to Recent times. Whole ones are rare.

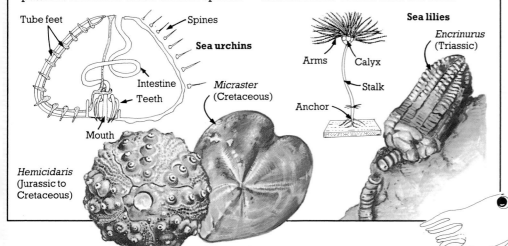

Tube feet

Spines

Sea urchins

Intestine

Teeth

Mouth

Micraster (Cretaceous)

Hemicidaris (Jurassic to Cretaceous)

Sea lilies

Encrinurus (Triassic)

Arms

Calyx

Stalk

Anchor

Ammonites and belemnites (Cephalopods)

Ammonites are now extinct but they were common in the seas of Jurassic and Cretaceous times. The flat circular shell was divided into chambers, with the animal living in the last one. Air in the empty chambers gave buoyancy for swimming. The complicated growth lines, best seen on worn shells, are important identification features. Belemnites were rather like modern squids, and the strange bullet-shaped fossils we find were originally inside the soft-bodied animal.

Ammonites

The modern *Nautilus*, a relative of the ammonites.

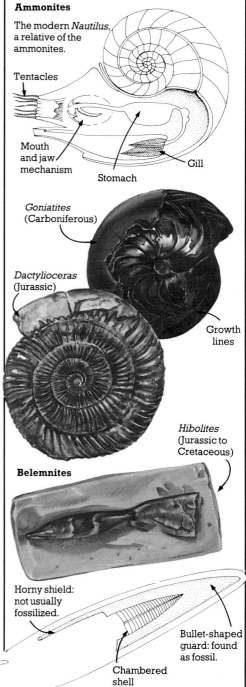

Tentacles

Mouth and jaw mechanism

Stomach

Gill

Goniatites (Carboniferous)

Dactylioceras (Jurassic)

Growth lines

Hibolites (Jurassic to Cretaceous)

Belemnites

Horny shield: not usually fossilized.

Chambered shell

Bullet-shaped guard: found as fossil.

Exploring the landscape

The sketches on these pages show some of the landscape features caused by different combinations of weather, climate and geology. There are many more, including landscapes created almost entirely by man, but once you learn how to 'read' the clues in the scenery you will be able to unravel the history of the landscape around you.

One of the most useful tools for exploring landscapes is a detailed map like those made by the Ordnance Survey. These show the shape of the land and the main rock outcrops as well as roads, tracks and footpaths and other interesting features like old railways, mines and quarries.

Making a geology map

Once you have learned to recognize the main rock types, and have become used to 'reading' the landscape around you, try making your own geology map. Work on tracing paper fixed securely over the Ordnance Survey map of your area.

Special equipment

To measure the slope of the rocks beds you will need a *clinometer*. You can make one easily from a rectangular block of wood, a 180-degree protractor, and a free-swinging pointer. But you will have to re-number the divisions from 0° in the centre to 90° at each end of the horizontal.

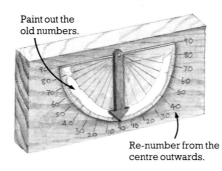

Paint out the old numbers.

Re-number from the centre outwards.

Place your clinometer on a bedding plane and move it until you get the maximum slope. This is the DIP of the rocks. You will also need a *compass* to measure the direction of dip. The line at right-angles to the dip is called the STRIKE of the rocks.

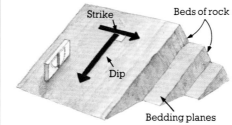

Strike

Beds of rock

Dip

Bedding planes

How to map the rocks

Start by heading for high ground. The strike of the rock beds often shows up in the landscape as ridges or bands of exposed rock. Then, if you walk *across* the strike, you will cross each rock layer in turn. The scene below is what you would see from 'Viewpoint rock'.

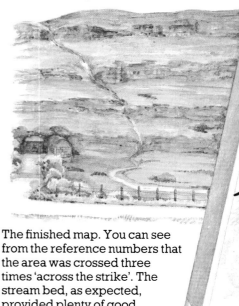

The finished map. You can see from the reference numbers that the area was crossed three times 'across the strike'. The stream bed, as expected, provided plenty of good outcrops. Later, all the definite contacts (solid lines) were joined up with dotted lines and the different rocks were coloured in. 'Shorthand' terms (l/st = limestone; s/st = sandstone) are used on the map.

The Matterhorn is a spectacular example of a peak carved by the action of frost and glaciers.

Weak or shattered rocks in the centre of a fold may be worn away by waves to form a cliff cave.

Sandstone headlands with horizontal bedding may be carved into arches which then collapse leaving tall 'sea stacks'.

Rounded masses of rock with deeply weathered joints are typical of granite moorland scenery. They are called 'tors'.

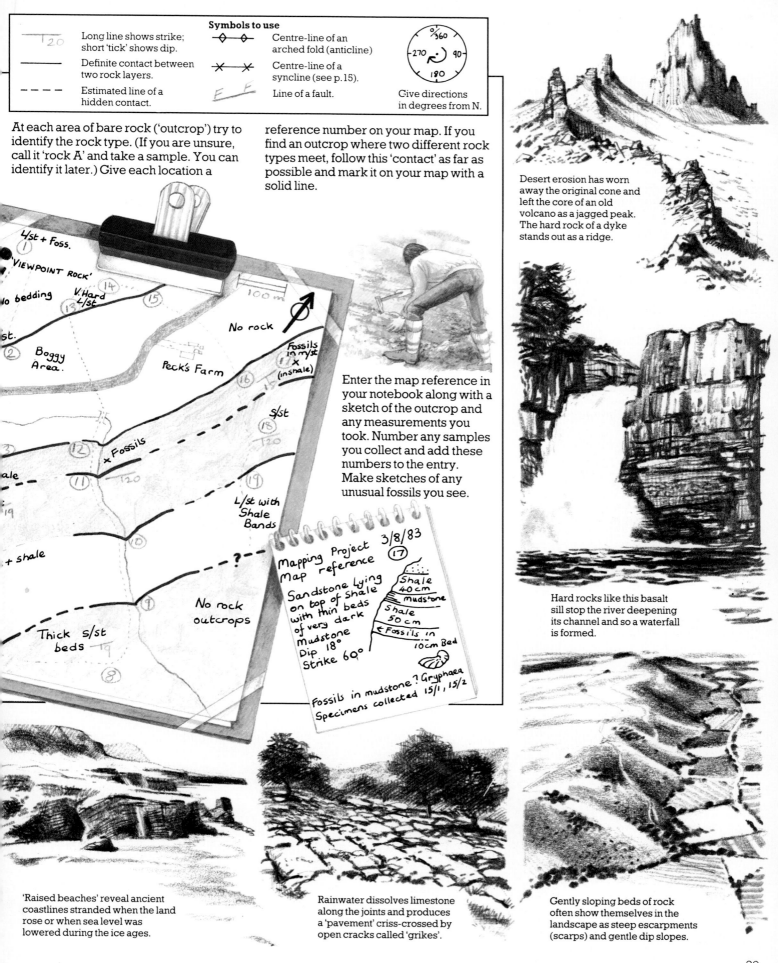

Symbols to use

⊤20	Long line shows strike; short 'tick' shows dip.	◇—◇	Centre-line of an arched fold (anticline)	
—	Definite contact between two rock layers.	✕—✕	Centre-line of a syncline (see p.15).	
- - - -	Estimated line of a hidden contact.	F—F	Line of a fault.	Give directions in degrees from N.

At each area of bare rock ('outcrop') try to identify the rock type. (If you are unsure, call it 'rock A' and take a sample. You can identify it later.) Give each location a reference number on your map. If you find an outcrop where two different rock types meet, follow this 'contact' as far as possible and mark it on your map with a solid line.

Desert erosion has worn away the original cone and left the core of an old volcano as a jagged peak. The hard rock of a dyke stands out as a ridge.

Enter the map reference in your notebook along with a sketch of the outcrop and any measurements you took. Number any samples you collect and add these numbers to the entry. Make sketches of any unusual fossils you see.

Notes on map:

⊥St + Foss.
'VIEWPOINT ROCK'
No bedding
V. Hard L/st
13 14 15
No rock
Boggy Area.
Peck's Farm
Fossils in m/st ✕ (in shale)
No rock
16
S/st
18 ⊤20
✕ Fossils
⊤20
L/st with Shale Bands
+ shale
No rock outcrops
Thick s/st beds ⊤9
100 m

Notebook:
Mapping Project
Map reference 3/8/83
(17)
Sandstone lying on top of shale with thin beds of very dark mudstone
Dip 18°
Strike 60°
Shale 40 cm
mudstone
Shale 50 cm
← Fossils in 10cm Bed
Fossils in mudstone? Gryphaea
Specimens collected 15/1, 15/2

Hard rocks like this basalt sill stop the river deepening its channel and so a waterfall is formed.

'Raised beaches' reveal ancient coastlines stranded when the land rose or when sea level was lowered during the ice ages.

Rainwater dissolves limestone along the joints and produces a 'pavement' criss-crossed by open cracks called 'grikes'.

Gently sloping beds of rock often show themselves in the landscape as steep escarpments (scarps) and gentle dip slopes.

29

The geologist at work

Professional geologists are involved in many activities – from laboratory research into rocks and fossils, to oil and mineral exploration in the most far-flung parts of the world. Geological research has helped set up early-warning systems to protect against the devastating tidal waves caused by submarine earthquakes; and studies of deep rock layers may one day help us make more use of the earth's internal heat as a source of energy. Geologists also play an important role in big engineering projects – in finding the best places to build dams and bridges for example, and in helping to plan tunnels for roads and hydroelectric schemes.

Rocks in brilliant colour

Even the dullest-looking rock may burst into rainbow colours when viewed under a geologist's microscope. A thin slice of rock is ground down until it is transparent and is then viewed using polarized light.

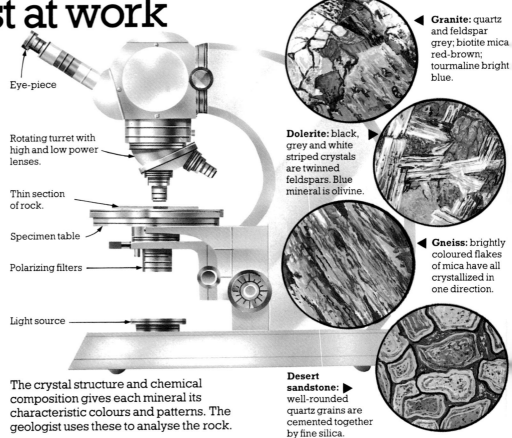

Eye-piece

Rotating turret with high and low power lenses.

Thin section of rock.

Specimen table

Polarizing filters

Light source

The crystal structure and chemical composition gives each mineral its characteristic colours and patterns. The geologist uses these to analyse the rock.

◄ **Granite:** quartz and feldspar grey; biotite mica red-brown; tourmaline bright blue.

Dolerite: black, grey and white striped crystals are twinned feldspars. Blue mineral is olivine.

◄ **Gneiss:** brightly coloured flakes of mica have all crystallized in one direction.

Desert sandstone: ▶ well-rounded quartz grains are cemented together by fine silica.

Prospecting methods

Geologists use several different exploration methods but three of the most important make use of shock waves passing through rock layers; differences in density of different rocks and mineral deposits; and the natural magnetism of some rocks.

Seismic methods use explosions or mechanical 'thumpers' to send shock waves through the rocks. These are reflected back to receivers on the surface and the trace, called a seismograph, reveals the hidden structures of the deep rock layers.

Gravity surveys measure the small differences in gravity caused by lighter or denser rocks lying under the earth's surface. The survey shown below has revealed a salt dome rising up through sedimentary rocks – a promising place to look for oil.

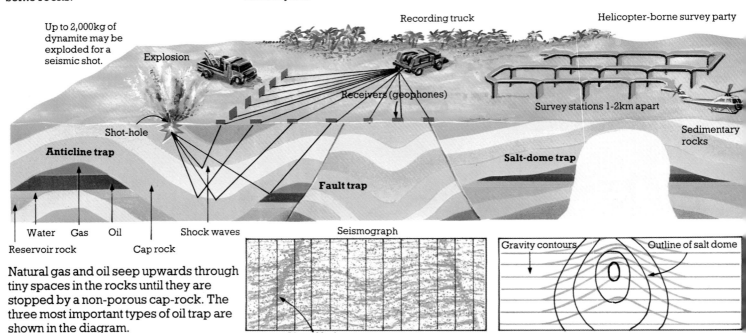

Up to 2,000kg of dynamite may be exploded for a seismic shot.

Recording truck

Helicopter-borne survey party

Explosion

Receivers (geophones)

Survey stations 1-2km apart

Sedimentary rocks

Anticline trap

Shot-hole

Fault trap

Salt-dome trap

Water Gas Oil

Reservoir rock   Cap rock

Shock waves

Seismograph

Gravity contours   Outline of salt dome

Natural gas and oil seep upwards through tiny spaces in the rocks until they are stopped by a non-porous cap-rock. The three most important types of oil trap are shown in the diagram.

Line of fault

Tsunami warning!

Huge 'tidal waves', more correctly called tsunamis, result from submarine earthquakes. Far out at sea they may be less than a metre high and 150km apart, but they can travel at up to 800kph! When they hit shallow water they can rear up to 40m high and do immense damage to coastal towns. Seismographs sited all round the Pacific Ocean record earth tremors and enable scientists to predict when waves will arrive.

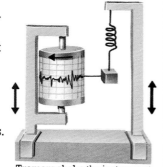

Tremors shake the instrument frame while the weight remains almost still. The trace is recorded on a rotating drum.

Japan

Hawaii

25
20
15
Arrival time (hours)
10
5

11,200km

Earthquake centre ✕

The search for oil

Drilling for oil is big business. It began on land, then moved into coastal waters, and finally into deeper waters like the North Sea. It is a high-technology world in which drilling, and installing the huge production platforms, completes the work started years earlier by exploration geologists.

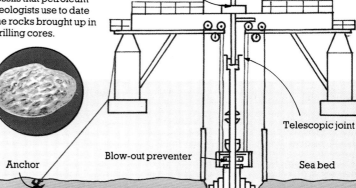

Foraminifera ('forams') (above) and ostracods (below) are among the most important of the microscopically small fossils that petroleum geologists use to date the rocks brought up in drilling cores.

Drill derrick

Turntable

Telescopic joint

Blow-out preventer

Sea bed

Anchor

Borehole casing

Rock layers

Drill 'string' (made up of 9-metre lengths of pipe).

Drill bit

Magnetic surveys are often carried out using airborne equipment that makes a continuous recording of the earth's magnetic field. Magnetic rocks, like the important iron ore magnetite, show up as high points on the print-out. Large scale regional surveys like this will often be followed up with more detailed surveys by ground parties if there are signs of useful ore deposits.

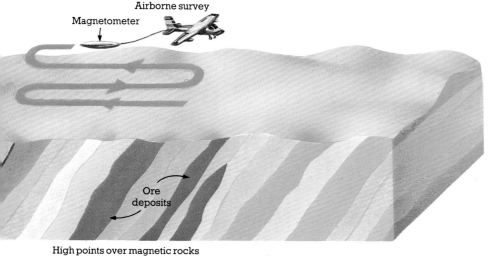

Airborne survey

Magnetometer

Ore deposits

High points over magnetic rocks

Other methods include measurements of how well the surface rocks can conduct electrical currents, and the use of Geiger counters and other even more sensitive instruments to search for important radio-active minerals like uranium and thorium.

The 'business end' of the drill string is the bit – for its size, one of the most expensive parts of the whole rig. Modern drilling can bore through 300m of soft rock an hour.

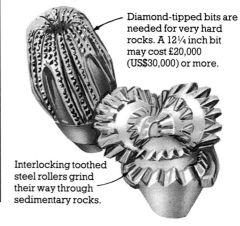

Diamond-tipped bits are needed for very hard rocks. A 12¼ inch bit may cost £20,000 (US$30,000) or more.

Interlocking toothed steel rollers grind their way through sedimentary rocks.

31

Index

First published in 1983 by
Usborne Publishing Ltd, Usborne House,
83-85 Saffron Hill, London EC1N 8RT
Copyright © 2007, 1994, 1983 Usborne Publishing Ltd.

The name Usborne and the devices 💡 🎈 are Trade Marks of Usborne Publishing Ltd.

Printed in Belgium.